One Peaceful Universe

Macrobiotic Cosmology and the Quest for Peace

EDWARD ESKO

FOREWORD BY ALEX JACK

Amberwaves Press

"Today's scientists have substituted mathematics for experiments, and wander off through equation after equation as they build a structure that has no relation to reality."
—NIKOLA TESLA

"If the facts don't fit the theory, change the facts."
—ALBERT EINSTEIN

One Peaceful Universe
Macrobiotic Cosmology and the Quest for Peace

Contents

One Peaceful Universe: Macrobiotic Cosmology and the Quest for Peace
From a lecture at the Macrobiotic Summer Conference
Copyright © 2017 Edward Esko
Foreword Copyright © 2017 by Alex Jack

ISBN-13: 978-1543158939
ISBN-10: 1543158935

Published by Amberwaves Press, a division of Planetary Health, Inc., a 501 (c)(3) non-profit organization
P.O. Box 487
Becket, MA 01223
Amberwaves.org
MacrobioticSummerConference.com

First Edition April 2017

Foreword

Van Gogh's *Wheat Field with Cypresses*

Creation myths reveal the heart and soul of a culture or civilization. The Big Bang, the modern creation myth, is a product of the nuclear age. It mirrors the catastrophic misuse of technology and power that culminated in the atomic bombing of Japan, the race to develop the H-bomb during the Cold War, and nuclear accidents in the Soviet Union and other countries.

The Big Bang reinforces the modern view that we live in a violent, chaotic world. It implies that there is no higher purpose or design to life beyond survival and that wild, explosive thoughts, extreme emotions, and destructive behaviors are normal. By analogy, it even sanctifies burdening posterity with a legacy of millions and billions of years of lethal nuclear waste in the way that cosmos background radiation from the primordial explosion is said to ripple through the firmament forever.

In *One Peaceful Universe*, Edward Esko challenges this paradigm. Building on ancient wisdom and the macrobiotic teachings of George Ohsawa and Michio Kushi, he presents an alternative, strikingly elegant, and entirely peaceful view of the cosmos and our place in it.

He shows that the Big Bang, black holes, dark matter, dark energy, and the thermonuclear sun are mathematical constructs and have no independent reality. The Big Bang, in particular, is a matter of faith, not scientific fact. It is not falsifiable—the bottom line for proving any scientific hypothesis.

The Big Bang, cosmic inflation, and other abstract concepts, as he suggests, arise from the modern way of eating high in meat, sugar, and other extremes. In contrast, a traditional diet centered on rice, wheat, and other whole cereal grains and predominantly plant-quality foods, views the world as an orderly, purposeful, and joyful whole.

In these pages, you will be introduced to yin and yang, Ki energy, the electric sun, fractal patterns in nature, and spiral waves and vibrations that form the invisible constitution to the universe and all of its wondrous manifestations. As Edward shows, a primary channel for receiving the energy of heaven and earth is whole grains. Unique among plants, they evolved *awns*—long, sensitive antennae—that collect, gather, and radiate the universal streaming energy of the heavens above and the subtle rhythms of the earth below.

By eating grains, we not only become more calm and peaceful. Our focus shifts from mundane personal concerns to planetary and celestial realms, and we discover the common dream of humanity.

Reconnecting with our eternal spiritual roots in the starry heavens is essential if we are to endure as a species and create a world of lasting health and peace. Like the serene, expressionistic swirls filling a Van Gogh canvas, *One Peaceful Universe* points the way.

Alex Jack
President Planetary Health

Creation Myths

Do we live in a peaceful universe, or do we not live in a peaceful universe? Unfortunately, our species, our human species is not very peaceful, especially at present. Every day there is war and violence all over the planet. Also the threat of giant war is constantly there, beyond local and individual violence.

Our goal in macrobiotics is One Peaceful World. In order to change our current not peaceful world into a peaceful world, we must awaken to the universe as it is. Hopefully we can begin to discover that the universe is in fact a very peaceful universe and that it is we who are out of touch with that universe.

Big Bang

Let's start with the most common stories about how the universe came into being. While getting ready for tonight's lecture, I watched a BBC documentary titled, "The Big Bang."

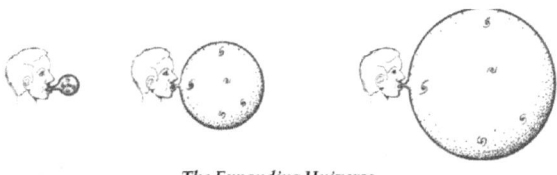

The Expanding Universe

The show presented the big bang theory together with a variety of other explanations. The big bang represents one extreme of the spectrum of creation myths. Do you think this theory originated in the West or in the East? It is very Western. The person who came up with the big bang was a Belgian priest. His dream was to find a scientific theory that matched the Book of Genesis. He stated that from nothing, from an infinitesimal point known as a "singularity," a giant explosion arose, throwing out all the matter in the universe. That explosion produced galaxies, stars, and planets; the entire known universe. People believe that the universe is expanding as a result of the big bang. If the universe is expanding, that expansion had to have started somewhere, so subscribers of the big bang march that process backwards, stating that the universe must have originated at a single point in time and space. The consensus is that the big bang took place about thirteen billion years ago.

As we see, this theory is stating that we all originated in violence. Everything we see today, including all of us, everything had a violent origin, a huge explosion. The big bang represents typical Western thinking.

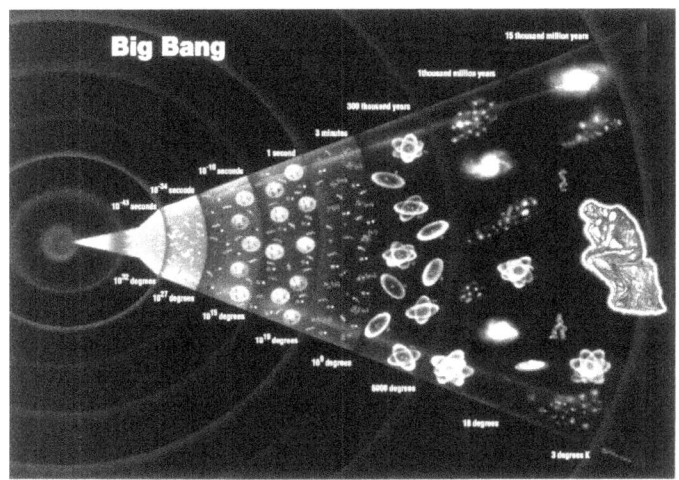

Inflation

One of the weaknesses of the big bang is the inability to answer the question "what was there before the big bang?" The answer to this is often "nothing." According to one theory, however, something known as "the inflation" was there before the big bang. (An opposite theory [cosmic inflation] states that the inflation was the immediate aftereffect of the big bang.)

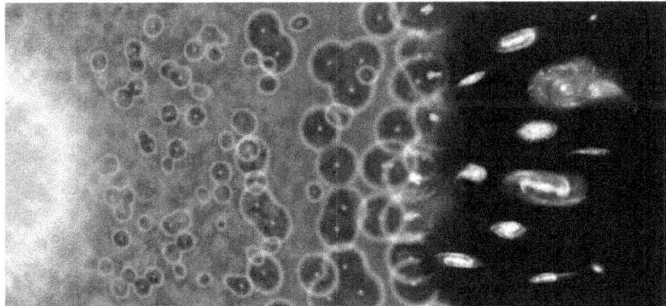

Cosmic inflation is a theory of exponential expansion of space in the early universe. The inflation was thought to last from 10^{-36} seconds to between 10^{-33} and 10^{-32} seconds after the big bang

The "before the big bang" interpretation is known as "eternal inflation," and leads to the concept of a multiverse, containing multiple universes. The model used to describe this is Swiss cheese (see above.) Within the inflation are many universes, created by multiple big bangs, like holes in Swiss cheese. Trillions of universes are thought to exist within the inflation, which is sometimes described as being infinite.

Big Bounce/Big Crunch

A hydrogen bomb, for me, was puny compared to the Big Bang—the creation of the universe. That's what I really wanted to work on—the nature of the universe itself, and that's what I do for a living. —Michio Kaku

As we go toward the East, we encounter creation stories proposed by theorists from India. Indian cosmologists believe that yes, the big bang occurred, creating the entire universe, but that there had to be something there before the big bang. These cosmologists believe that what existed before the big bang derives from the Indian philosophy of karma; never-ending cycles of yin and yang, or expansion and contraction.

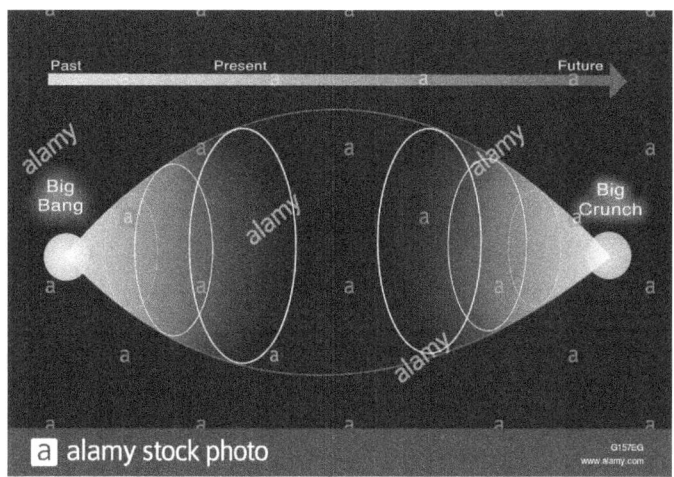

What do you think they say was there before the big bang? If the big bang produced expansion, which is yin, it must have been preceded by cosmic contraction, or yang. They say the big bang followed the contraction of the previous universe. That contraction is known as the "big crunch." Once contraction reached a peak, the universe then began to expand. This is referred to as the "big bounce." However, questions as to how, why, and when these events occurred remain unanswered.

An Open Letter
To the Scientific Community

All of these mainstream theories, as varied as they are, from East to West and back again, embrace the big bang. There is, however, a growing movement challenging the hegemony of big bang. Nevertheless, the big bang continues to dominate mainstream scientific thinking, including the funding for academic research and publication in scientific journals. Any research that attempts to go outside the big bang usually does not receive funding and is rejected for publication. The big bang has thus become modern dogma that stifles freethinking and objective research.

A group of scientists published a summary of the challenges to the big bang in "An Open Letter to the Scientific Community" (*New Scientist*, May 22, 2004). Its contents are highly revealing.

> The big bang today relies on a growing number of hypothetical entities, things that we have never observed—inflation, dark matter and dark energy are the most prominent examples. Without them, there would be a fatal contradiction between the observations made by astronomers and the predictions of the big bang theory. In no other field of physics would this continual recourse to new hypothetical objects be accepted as a way of bridging the gap between theory and observation. It would, at the least, raise serious questions about the validity of the underlying theory.

But the big bang theory can't survive without these fudge factors. Without the hypothetical inflation field, the big bang does not predict the smooth, isotropic cosmic background radiation that is observed, because there would be no way for parts of the universe that are now more than a few degrees away in the sky to come to the same temperature and thus emit the same amount of microwave radiation.

Without some kind of dark matter, unlike any that we have observed on Earth despite 20 years of experiments, big-bang theory makes contradictory predictions for the density of matter in the universe. Inflation requires a density 20 times larger than that implied by big bang nucleosynthesis, the theory's explanation of the origin of the light elements. And without dark energy, the theory predicts that the universe is only about 8 billion years old, which is billions of years younger than the age of many stars in our galaxy.

What is more, the big bang theory can boast of no quantitative predictions that have subsequently been validated by observation. The successes claimed by the theory's supporters consist of its ability to retrospectively fit observations with a steadily increasing array of adjustable parameters, just as the old Earth-centered cosmology of Ptolemy needed layer upon layer of epicycles.

Yet the big bang is not the only framework available for understanding the history of the universe. Plasma cosmology and the steady-state model both hypothesize an evolving universe without beginning or end. These and other alternative approaches can also explain the basic phenomena of the cosmos, including the abundances of light elements, the generation of large-scale structure, the cosmic background radiation, and how the redshift of far-away galaxies increases with distance. They have even predicted new phenomena that were subsequently observed, something the big bang has failed to do.

Supporters of the big bang theory may retort that these theories do not explain every cosmological observation. But that is scarcely surprising, as their development has been severely hampered by a complete lack of funding. Indeed, such questions and alternatives cannot even now be freely discussed and examined. An open exchange of ideas is lacking in most mainstream conferences. Whereas Richard Feynman could say that "science is the culture of doubt," in cosmology today doubt and dissent are not tolerated, and young scientists learn to remain silent if they have something negative to say about the standard big bang model. Those who doubt the big bang fear that saying so will cost them their funding.

Even observations are now interpreted through this biased filter, judged right or wrong depending on whether or not they support the big bang. So discordant data on red shifts, lithium and helium abundances, and galaxy distribution, among other topics, are ignored or ridiculed. This reflects a growing dogmatic mindset that is alien to the spirit of free scientific inquiry.

Today, virtually all financial and experimental resources in cosmology are devoted to big bang studies. Funding comes from only a few sources, and all the peer-review committees that control them are dominated by supporters of the big bang. As a result, the dominance of the big bang within the field has become self-sustaining, irrespective of the scientific validity of the theory.

Giving support only to projects within the big bang framework undermines a fundamental element of the scientific method—the constant testing of theory against observation. Such a restriction makes unbiased discussion and research impossible. To redress this, we urge those agencies that fund work in cosmology to set aside a significant fraction of their funding for investigations into alternative theories and observational contradictions of the big bang. To avoid bias, the peer review committee that allocates such funds could be composed of astronomers and physicists from outside the field of cosmology.

Allocating funding to investigations into the big bang's validity, and its alternatives, would allow the scientific process to determine our most accurate model of the history of the universe.

The big bang is not actually a theory. It is a hypothesis. A hypothesis is a mental construct that must be tested and confirmed before it qualifies as a theory. There is no way to test or prove the big bang. As we see in the above critique of modern cosmology, there is huge controversy within the scientific community due to the rigid adherence to the big bang and the refusal of mainstream science to investigate or fund alternate hypotheses.

Also, as we have seen above, major shortcomings have appeared within the big bang. Theoretical physicists, who are not like pioneers such as Rutherford or Maxwell, who conducted actual laboratory experiments, but who are more like mathematicians and computer programmers, dream up so-called "fudge factors" to account for these weaknesses. These inventions include "dark matter," "dark energy," and "black hole."

Thermonuclear Sun

Another tenet of modern cosmology states that our Sun is a huge thermonuclear reactor. In 1920, mathematician Arthur Eddington developed the idea that nuclear energy was being released in the Sun's core. This idea gained credence following the creation of atomic weapons in the 1940s, including the Manhattan Project, the explosion of atomic bombs over Hiroshima and Nagasaki, and the detonation of the first hydrogen bomb in 1950.

"A new consensus arose, a conviction that only a fusion reactor at the Sun's core could explain the Sun's powerful emissions of heat and light. And now every student in the sciences reads about the hypothesis as fact." (David Talbott, *Discovering the Electric Sun*, Thunderbolts.info.)

What is the Sun, according to this concept? What is the driving force that powers the Sun and creates its energy? That driving force is gravity. Isaac Newton started this concept. What is the idea of gravity? Everything in space, every body in space, is pulling matter in towards itself, a force known as "gravitational" force.

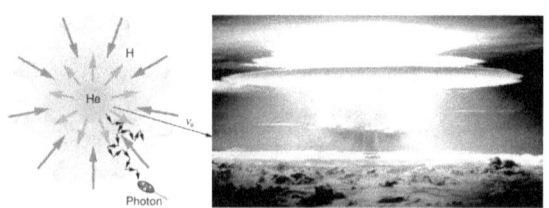

Current view of the Sun

Thus, according to the theory of gravity, the Sun, being gigantic, has huge gravitational force, creating at the center incredibly high temperature and pressure. These high temperatures and pressures force the primary element in the Sun, hydrogen, to fuse with itself, and form a new element, helium.

According to the modern view, the fusion of atoms, such as that thought to occur in the Sun, occurs only under extreme and violent conditions. The earthly equivalent of this is the hydrogen bomb. The hydrogen bomb has isotopes of hydrogen at its core. An atomic bomb is exploded to force these isotopes to fuse with each other, releasing tremendous energy in the process. According to the thermonuclear Sun hypothesis, a similar process of nuclear fusion is constantly occurring at the center of the Sun.

In other words, the Sun is a continuously exploding hydrogen bomb. So at the core of our life, at the very core or our existence, is an incredibly violent event. In a similar vein, the modern view of the creation of the universe states that the universe itself was created in an incredibly violent event known as the big bang. These are the current ruling paradigms.

As we can see, according to the modern view, our universe is an incredibly violent place. Not peaceful at all. Unless we change that view, we won't be able to have a peaceful world. If violence is at the very core of our cosmology, our view of life and the universe, it is very difficult to achieve peace. Therefore it is essential that we modify these concepts and begin to see the universe as it is.

Ki Cosmology

Perhaps we must turn to Far Eastern cosmology to see things as they are. The ancient Chinese character for Ki, or life energy, accurately depicts the never-ending process through which our universe comes into being. The pattern of creation is revealed throughout nature. Ferns and other plants offer clear examples. What do we see when we look at a fern? We see one main stream of energy dividing into two. Two streams come out, and each divides again into two. These divisions continually separate into two until we reach the microscopic scale.

That pattern is known in macrobiotics as yin and yang, in which one becomes two; two become four; four become eight, and so on into infinity. In modern terms, that pattern is known as "fractal" division. From the macroscopic view, we have large streams of energy continually dividing, becoming smaller and smaller. From the microscopic view, there are patterns that continually repeat, becoming larger and larger.

If you Google "fractals in nature," you'll discover countless examples. Fractal patterns represent the pattern of creation itself. They reveal how the universe continually manifests. Thus, fractals can be found everywhere, in all things. The creation of the universe through fractal division is depicted in the character for Ki. The outer portion of the character depicts the creation of the universe as energy streaming out from infinity. It shows the endless process of the universe coming into being. The lines in the inner portion of the character depict the image of a rice plant.

Ice crystals are a perfect example of fractal patterns

The universe, through its endless manifestation, originating in pure energy, takes the form of rice or other cereal grains in the plant kingdom. Human beings are the counterparts to cereal grains in the animal kingdom. All grains have tiny hair like projections coming out from the top. In corn, for example, these projections are known as the corn "silk." In other grains, such as barley, rice, and wheat, these projections are known as "awns." What do they remind you of?

The awns point upward toward the cosmos. Like tiny antennae, they channel the energy of the universe itself. During the day they channel energy from the Sun. At night, they channel energy from the night sky, including the billions of stars in our own Milky Way.

In the case of rice, as the plant matures in late summer, the grains bend down toward the earth. Prior to that, the grains point upward toward heaven. Once they reach maturity and start to bend down, the awns begin channeling the energy of the earth.

Heirloom rice (above) has awns, while hybridized (awnless) rice does not. The appearance of grains at the head of the plant duplicates the pattern of fractal creation found throughout the universe

It is only when the grains become saturated with heaven's energy, becoming heavier and heavier, that they bend down and begin receiving energy from the earth. The energies of heaven and earth converge in each grain and are stored there like the information stored in a microchip. That is why we say that grain is highly charged with life energy.

By eating grains, especially heirloom varieties that contain the awns at the end of each grain, we are receiving energy directly from heaven and earth. (Hybridized, awnless grains lack this natural connection.) The energy from the entirety of nature is the energy of peace, harmony, and balance. Eating grain imparts that peaceful energy while putting you in touch with universal consciousness. In contrast, the energy coming from factory farmed cattle and other animal food is not peaceful at all. It is far removed from universal consciousness. Think about the living conditions of these unfortunate creatures, and also imagine their manner of death. Basing the diet on factory farmed animal foods makes it difficult to see the peaceful reality of the universe as it truly is.

Grain is at the center of the universe's evolution. The appearance of our human species, characterized by our unique human form, posture, and highly developed consciousness, is the result of eating cereal grains. The inner lines in the character for Ki reveal the importance of rice and other cereals, and also depict the universal pattern of creation.

The vertical and horizontal lines are the first to appear. They represent the appearance of the two primary forces—yin and yang—from one infinity. The intersection of yin and yang produces four appearances, up and down and left and right. We see that in the fractal pattern of the fern, one stream of energy divides into two, left and right, and these streams again divide into two. That process continues until each cell of the plant is formed. In the universe, one divides into two, two into four, four into eight, and so on until the universe and everything within it comes into being.

Our Fractal Body

The human body is a microcosm of the universe as a whole. We see fractal patterns in both the visible and invisible form of the body. They reflect the patterns found in the universe at large. There are two big poles in the human body. One is at our North Pole on top of the head. It is positively charged. The opposite pole, located in the genital region, is negatively charged. The source of energy animating the North Pole is force coming down from the universe, showering onto the surface of the planet. We call that "heaven's force." The source of the energy coming in to the lower body is the rotation of the earth. We call that "earth's force." The energy of the earth is the expanding force that causes hair to grow on the head and plants to branch upward. Heaven's force is the opposite: it makes rain fall to the earth. It makes things become solid and dense.

Between the two opposite poles is a strong charge, like an electric arc arising between anode and cathode. That charge comprises our core of life energy. Seven highly charged nodes—known as chakras—arise along that invisible channel. Energy gathers in the chakras. They are highly charged. Energy bubbles up from this central core toward the surface of the body, forming invisible lines or channels. These are known as "meridians." Obeying the law of fractal division, the meridians continually divide into smaller streams, creating numerous microscopic branches.

At the end of each branch is a tiny spiral of energy, which we can't see. We have trillions of tiny spirals. Each one is alive, charged with life energy. These are the body's cells. Every cell is receiving life energy from the meridians, chakras, and ultimately from heaven and earth. This system is invisible. We can't see it.

Parallel to this is another fractal system, originating from the opposite energy of the earth. It also branches into tiny divisions. Big channels divide into smaller and smaller channels, ending, like the energy system, in trillions of tiny structures, known as capillaries that surround the cells. This system merges with the invisible energy system to form the substance of the body. We refer to it as the circulatory system. The circulatory vessels carry oxygen and nutrients to the cells and provide each cell with material substance: mineral, protein, fat, and water.

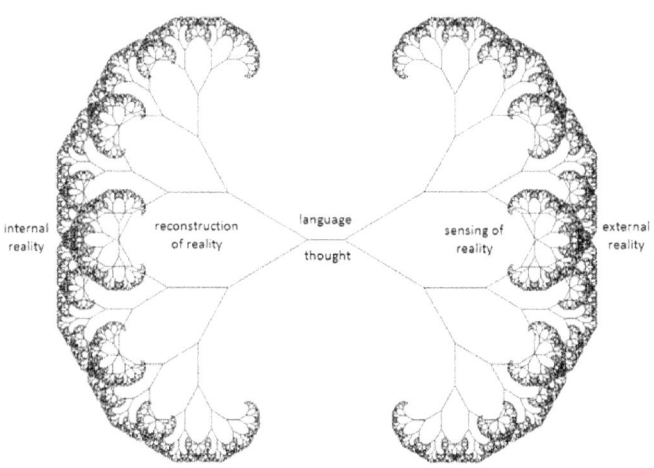

Fractal pattern of human brain. Neurons are condensed spirals that form along fractal branched nerve fibers. Fractals are found throughout the body's organs and systems

We also take in air through our fractal-structured respiratory system. One stem, branches into two, which then branch continuously until tiny air sacs are formed. The nervous system, liver, spleen, pancreas, kidneys, and other organs and structures all display fractal patterns. Our body is a fractal entity that fuses the energies of heaven and earth.

Our Fractal Universe

Not only are fractals found in our bodies and in the immediate environment, they are also found in the largest structures in the universe. The discovery of these giant structures may invalidate the big bang hypothesis and lead to a new understanding of the origin of the universe.

One of these structures is known as the Sloan great wall, a supercluster of galaxies 1.36 billion light years long. Discovered in 2003, such a structure would require 250 billion years to form. This is only the most recent of these discoveries; others were made over the past several decades.

What are these giant structures? Their pattern is the same as that found in the body and in nature; the same as in ferns, our circulatory and other systems, and our chakras and meridians of energy. They are giant streams of energy that divide continuously in a fractal pattern, becoming smaller and smaller until they end in highly condensed spirals of energy. They are found all over the universe.

Astronomers have identified seven discrete levels or layers of these structures, ranging from the microcosmic to the macrocosmic, from earth to the universe as a whole:

7. The observable universe

6. A supercluster (ours is known as the Laniakea Supercluster)

5. A local group of galaxies (ours includes the Milky Way and Andromeda galaxies)

4. The galactic realm (the Milky Way)

3. The solar neighborhood (interstellar space)
2. The solar system
1. Planet earth

What are the tiny spirals at the end of each of the fractal divisions? From the point of view of the macrocosm, they are tiny. From our point of view, they are gigantic. On the largest scale, the fractal formed spirals are the superclusters containing billions of local groups of galaxies. Next, within the local groups are numerous individual galaxies, and within each galaxy are billions of solar systems. Within the solar systems are individual planets, their satellites, and various forms of debris such as asteroids and comets.

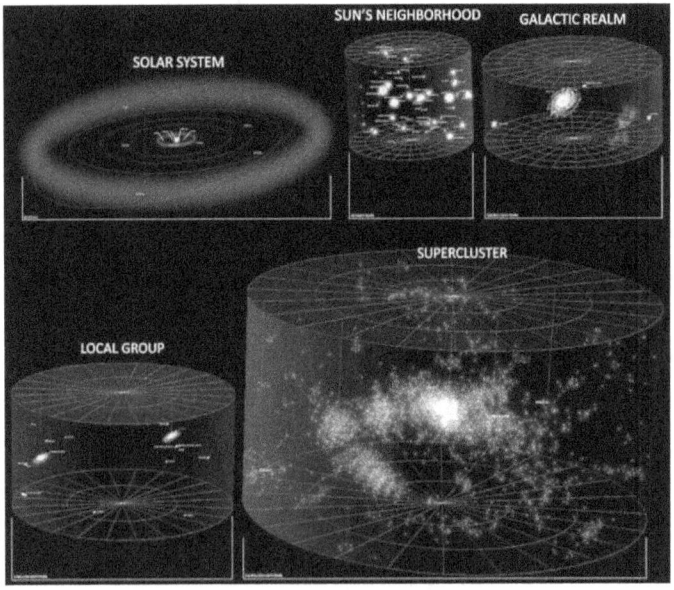

All of these structures obey the law of fractal, or yin and yang, division. They appear as either large currents or filaments of energy and as huge spiral formations.

26

These structures are not isolated from each other but are connected, like the grains of rice on the rice plant or the organs and systems of the body. The gravitational model says that all bodies in the universe are isolated. They are independent islands. In reality, however, everything in the universe is part of an interdependent system, just like the systems of the body.

When we see these fractals from the side, we observe a main stream that continually divides. When we see them from the top or from the front, we see spirally formed patterns. It depends on our perspective. This is like the particle and wave nature of light and subatomic particles. It is also like the fractal pattern seen in the formation of rice and other cereal plants in which the central stem divides and ends in compact grains.

The discovery of these giant structures seems to invalidate the big bang. The big bang states that the universe began about 13 billion years ago. The largest of these structures are much older than that. Moreover, even the largest known structures—the superclusters—are infinitesimal in relation to the universe at large. The universe may actually be much older and much larger than we imagine.

Is the Universe Expanding?

Another threat to the hegemony of the big bang is coming from a variety of challenges to the idea of an expanding universe. The big bang is founded on the expanding universe. The notion of an expanding universe is based on observation of "redshift" associated with stars and galaxies. Redshift is part of the familiar "Doppler effect." It applies to both sound and light waves.

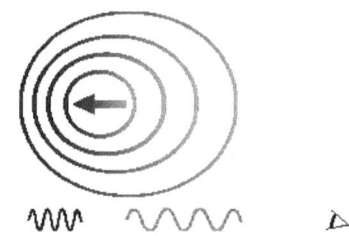

Source moving TOWARD observer
Wavelength decreasing,
Frequency increasing,
Observer experiencing BLUE shift.

Source moving AWAY from observer
Wavelength increasing,
Frequency decreasing,
Observer experiencing RED shift.

An example of the Doppler effect occurs when an ambulance siren moves toward an observer. As the siren approaches, the pitch becomes higher. As the siren passes, the pitch becomes lower. That occurs because the waves emitted from the siren as it moves toward the observer are compressed, causing their wavelengths to become shorter. Short waves produce higher pitch. In the case of light, short waves appear toward the blue end of the spectrum. (That phenomenon is known as "blueshift.")

On the other hand, when the source is moving away from the observer, waves are stretched or elongated; they change into long waves that have a lower pitch or appear on the red end of the spectrum (redshift.)

Yang	Yin
Object moving toward	Object moving away
Incoming	Outgoing
Contraction	Expansion
Tension	Relaxation
Compressed wave	Elongated wave
Short wave	Long wave
High pitch	Low pitch
Blueshift	Redshift

The macrobiotic principle of yin and yang helps us understand the Doppler effect. When something is moving toward us it is moving in an incoming or yang direction. Waves produced by incoming sound or light are compressed or shortened (yang). Compressed sound or light waves produce yin, higher pitched sound or blue light. Waves that move away from us are stretched (yin), and produce lower pitch or red light (yang.) This is a perfect illustration of the law in which yang produces yin and yin produces yang.

This effect is fundamental to the concept of an expanding universe. The American astronomer, Edwin Hubble, noted that the light from distant galaxies shifted toward the red end of the spectrum. From that it was assumed that galaxies are moving away from each other, with the most distant galaxies moving away the fastest. This led to the concept that the universe itself must be expanding, even though Hubble himself was skeptical. He stated in 1947, "It seems likely that redshift may not be due to an expanding universe, and much of the speculations on the structure of the universe may require reexamination."

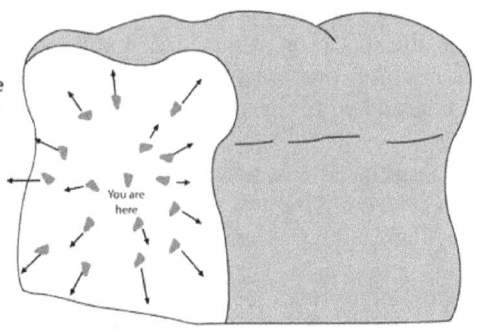

You are sitting on one raisin in the center of a rising loaf of raisin bread. You see every other raisin receding from you, and those further away are receding faster.

The "raisin bread" model of the expanding universe. This model overlooks the necessity of an opposite contracting force pushing in from outside, for example, the heat and energy generated by the oven that cause the bread to "rise" or expand

A powerful challenge to the expanding universe, and thus to the big bang, came to light with the discovery of quasars. These objects have a redshift greater than any other objects observed in the universe. Applying the redshift model, it was assumed that these objects were the most distant and moving away from us with the highest speed. And, although appearing dim, these objects were thought to possess the highest energy of any objects in the heavens.

These assumptions were thrown into question with the discoveries of the noted astronomer Halton Arp.

"In the 1960s, the astronomer Halton Arp, a highly respected authority on 'peculiar galaxies,' began documenting instances where low-redshifted galaxies and high-redshifted quasars were interacting, or even physically connected. This would mean that redshift signifies something other than an object's recessional velocity. [Recessional velocity is the rate at which an object is moving away from the observer.] If he was right, his observations were pointing to one of the biggest mistakes in the history of modern science." (*The Electric Universe—Big Bang?* Mikimar Publishing.)

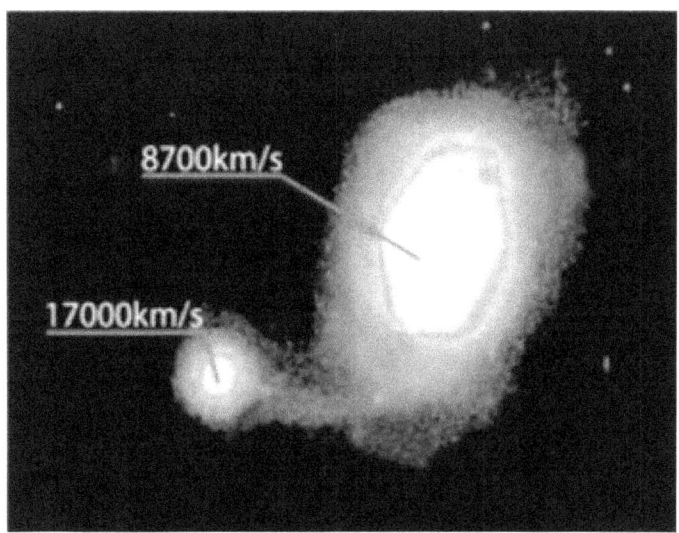

The high redshift quasar (lower left) seems to be attached to the low redshift galaxy (upper right) by a "bridge." That suggests quasars my not be as distant as once thought. Recently, a quasar was identified *in front* of a nearby galaxy

Recent observations seem to confirm Harp's hypothesis. In 2003 astronomers discovered a quasar with a high redshift located in front of a galaxy with a much lower redshift:

"On October 3, 2003, the big bang theory was falsified by direct observation. The galaxy NGC 7319 was measured to have a redshift of $z = 0.0225$. It is not uncommon for 'nearby' galaxies to have redshifts below $z = 1$. However, a quasar was located in front of NGC 7319's opaque gas clouds with a redshift of $z = 2.114$." (Stephen Smith, *Redshifts and Microwaves*, Thunderbolts.info.)

These discoveries challenge the assumption that the universe is expanding.

Our Peaceful Sun

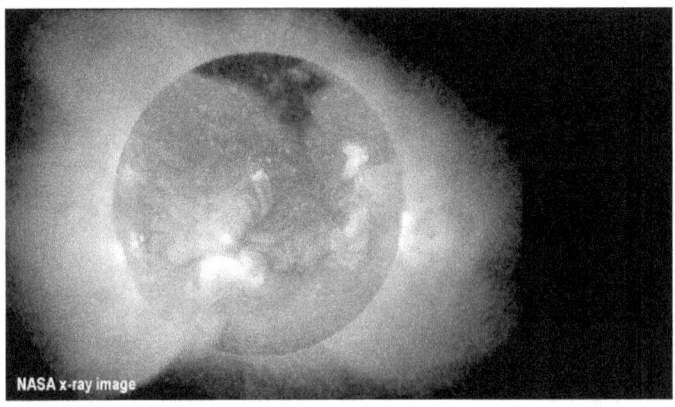

NASA x-ray image

As we saw in Chapter 3, today's scientific consensus is that the Sun is a thermonuclear reactor. Modern cosmologists believe the Sun is a continually exploding hydrogen bomb in which, under great temperature and pressure, hydrogen is being transmuted into helium. (Hydrogen is the first element, helium the second.)

The thermonuclear model is founded on Newton's idea of universal gravitation, in which the gravitational force of a star compresses its matter in on itself. As in a hydrogen bomb, tremendous centripetal or inward (yang) force produces great temperatures and pressures. These forces smash atoms into each other, causing them to fuse. This process releases tremendous energy, resulting in heat, light, charged particles, and radiation (yin).

In the gravitational model, the source of energy for the Sun is the gravitational force of the Sun itself. The Sun is pulling mass toward its center. The Sun will eventually exhaust its supply of nuclear fuel and then burn out.

However, the concept of a thermonuclear Sun is facing a serious challenge. The new model is based on studies of plasma and electricity as well as satellite observations such as those of Japan's Hinode spacecraft and NASAs fleet of Thermis spacecraft. It is also based on observations of the Sun's corona, solar wind, sunspots, penumbra, and dramatic occurrences such as solar flares, prominences, and coronal mass ejections.

The Electric Sun hypothesis states that the origin of the Sun's energy is not the Sun itself, but the electrically charged medium—the galaxy—that surrounds it. Thus, the Sun is not a thermonuclear reactor powered by gravity, but a gigantic conductor of electricity. Critics of the gravity powered, thermonuclear Sun point out that gravity is actually the weakest force in the universe—electrical energy is estimated to be 10^{39} power stronger than gravity.

Nearly 70 years ago, Dr. C.E.R. Bruce, an astronomer and electric researcher, presented a new hypothesis about the Sun. He suggested that the Sun was an electrical discharge phenomenon:

"It is not a coincidence that the photosphere has the appearance, the temperature and spectrum of an electric arc; it has arc characteristics because it is an electric arc, or a large number of arcs in parallel. These arcs quickly result in the neutralization of the accumulated space charge in their neighborhood and go out. They are not therefore stable discharges, but may rather be looked upon as transient sparks. Arcs thus continually appear and disappear. It is this coming and going which accounts for the observed granulation of the solar surface."

According to this hypothesis, most of the space in our galaxy contains plasma (electrically charged gas.) Plasmas are made up of electrons, which have a negative charge and ionized atoms, which have positive charge.

Every charged particle in the plasma has potential energy or voltage. The Sun is at the center of an immense plasma cell, called the *heliosphere* that stretches far out—several times the radius of Pluto. The radius is estimated to be 18 billion km or 122 times the distance of the earth to the Sun.

The Sun is positively charged in relation to the space around it. Negative electrons from space enter the Sun from the outside while positive ions exit the Sun, creating a plasma discharge like those seen in electric plasma laboratories.

The Sun may be powered, not from within itself, but from the electric currents that flow from our arm of the galaxy in toward the Sun. The Sun's positive charge causes it to act as the anode in a plasma discharge. The negative charge, or cathode, originates far out in space at the edge of the heliosphere, in a region known as the *heliopause*, which as we saw above, is about 18 billion km from the Sun. (For more on this, read *The Electric Universe*, by Wallace Thornhill and David Talbot, Mikimar Publishing, 2007.)

Keep in mind that the solar system is revolving around the center of the galaxy at enormous speed. The heliopause is located at the edge of this motion at the extreme periphery of the solar system. It generates high energy that complements and balances the electric charge of the central Sun.

The new model is consistent with the macrobiotic view that the energy powering the Sun originates not from the Sun itself, but from the periphery of the solar system and beyond into the galaxy itself. The Sun may not be a nuclear reactor, but the focus of a high-energy electric discharge.

The Cosmology of Peace

cos·mol·o·gy
käz'mäləjē/
noun
noun: **cosmology**

1. The science of the origin and development of the universe. Modern astronomy is dominated by the Big Bang theory, which brings together observational astronomy and particle physics.

2. An account or theory of the origin of the universe.

plural noun: **cosmologies**

Origin: Mid 17th century: from French *cosmologie* or modern Latin *cosmologia*, from Greek *kosmos* 'order, world' + *-logia* 'discourse.' *Source*: Google Search

Alternative views of the universe, for example that the big bang never happened and the electric Sun, are closer to macrobiotic cosmology than mainstream concepts like the big bang and thermonuclear Sun. In the future, the dominance of the big bang and other concepts based on a violent universe will be overturned. A new vision, more in line with the peaceful reality of existence, shall come to reign.

That new vision could very well come from the cosmology of macrobiotics, a cosmology that links all phenomena in a grand unification.

In macrobiotic cosmology, as defined by George Ohsawa and Michio Kushi, the universe is continually manifesting in the form of a logarithmic spiral originating in the infinite expansion. The oneness of infinity gives rise to space and time, beginning and end, front and back, and the countless sets of polarities that define our relative world. Polarization, which in macrobiotics we refer to as yin and yang, creates endless movement, energy, change, and evolution.

In essence, the universe is comprised of energy, waves, or vibrations that eventually condense into matter. Spirals form in an inward or centripetal direction. Pure, diffuse energy becomes increasingly yang or contracted, creating pre-atomic particles such as electrons, protons, and neutrons; the world of atoms or elements; the vegetable world; and finally, the world of animals and human beings. The process of creation occurs in a spiral with seven stages.

7. One infinity (the eternally non-manifest or non-being; the source of all manifestation and all being.)

6. Polarization (the two primary forces—yin and yang—that give rise to being or manifestation.)

5. Energy (the first appearance of being; endless movement in the form of contracting and expanding spirals, fractal filaments and currents, etc.

4. Preatomic particles (condensed spirals of energy that take the form of electrons, protons, etc. It is here that the giant plasma currents appear that give rise to superclusters, local groups of galaxies, and individual galaxies.)

3. Elements (further condensed and complex spirals of energy that take the form of stars, planets, comets, interstellar gas, etc.)

2. Plant life (further complex fractal spirals of energy with self-replicating abilities.)

1. Animal life, and ultimately human beings.

The human form and consciousness is the most condensed, complex, and free of all energy spirals found in the universe, with multiple interacting fractal structures, both visible and invisible. The fractals found in human physiology are internal and hidden, or yang; those appearing in the plant world are the opposite—external, exposed, and yin. They complement each other perfectly.

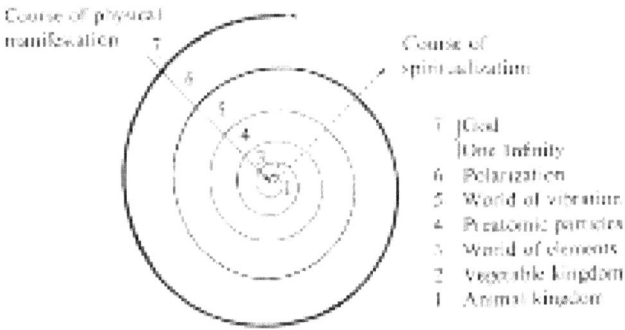

Spiral of materialization developed by Ohsawa and Kushi

In the macrobiotic view, the universe was not created at a fixed point in time, but is continually becoming manifest through what Ohsawa and Kushi named the "spiral of creation or materialization." The universe is at all times new. Galaxies, stars, and planets, appear, exist for a while, and then vanish in cosmic cycles governed by universal law. New galaxies, stars, and planets then appear and follow the same universal law. The universal law of change—yin changes into yang; and yang changes into yin—exists beyond time and space. The process of creation is going on throughout the universe at this very moment. The process has no beginning and no end.

Ohsawa understood that spirals form at the periphery, or outside, and wind inward toward the center. Here, they reverse course and begin an outward journey back toward the periphery. Galaxies exhibit this pattern, as does our solar system. Ohsawa, and later Michio Kushi, pointed out that the Sun's energy did not originate within the Sun itself, but from the periphery of the spiral at which the Sun is the center.

Proponents of the Electric Sun identify this spiral as the heliopause and agree that the energy that powers the Sun originates at the periphery (yin) and not at the center (yang.) They suggest that the energy powering the Sun is electrical and not gravitational or nuclear.

In macrobiotic cosmology, the solar system, galaxy, and universe itself are created from the outside in, and not from the inside out, as suggested by the big bang and gravitational (nuclear) Sun models. Even if we agree that electricity and magnetism, and not gravity, is the prime force of the universe, we need to progress beyond that to the origin of electricity and magnetism, which is the primary polarization of the universe, which we term yin and yang. And progressing beyond that, we arrive at the infinite oneness of life itself, beyond time and space, beyond the relative changing universe, yet forever giving rise to the relative changing universe. In order to realize a peaceful world, we must see the universe, as it is, an endlessly manifesting, orderly and peaceful reality.

Resources

Planetary Health/Amberwaves, PO Box 487, Becket MA 01223, 413-623-0012, www.amberwaves.org. A grassroots network devoted to preserving amber waves of grain and keeping America and the planet beautiful. Amberwaves is publisher of numerous books and a quarterly newsletter with articles by Edward Esko and Alex Jack. Planetary Health, a 501(c)(3) non-profit educational organization, sponsors the annual Macrobiotic Summer Conference in the Berkshires featuring leading teachers and authors from around the world.

Visit www.macrobioticsummerconference.com for further information.

Macrobiotics Today/**George Ohsawa Macrobiotic Foundation (GOMF)**, 1277 Marian Ave., Chico CA 95928, 800-232-2372, www.OhsawaMacrobiotics.com. GOMF is a macrobiotic publisher and educational center on the West Coast. *Macrobiotics Today* quarterly features articles by Edward Esko, Alex Jack, and other macrobiotic authors.

The Thunderbolts Project, www.thunderboltsinfo.com. A major online source for information about the Electric Sun and Electric Universe models. Publishes news updates, position papers, and sponsors annual conferences.

About the Author

Edward Esko is one of the world's most active contemporary macrobiotic teachers. Over the past four decades, he has lectured and counseled in Europe, Asia, Latin America, and throughout North America, including at the United Nations, and has written and edited numerous books and articles. Building on the teachings of George Ohsawa, Michio Kushi, and other macrobiotic pioneers, he has applied yin and yang—the universal principles of change and harmony—to helping solve issues of personal and planetary health. He has served as Vice President of the East West Foundation and Associate Director and Senior Faculty member at the Kushi Institute. He is the founder of macrobiotic-classroom.com and serves as Vice President of Planetary Health, Inc. His books include *Yin Yang Primer, Contemporary Macrobiotics, Rice Field Essays, Dandelion Essays*, *Ki: The Energy of Life*, *Opening Your Third Eye*, and *The Next Twenty Years*, as well as *Cool Fusion* and *Corking the Nuclear Genie,* coauthored with Alex Jack. Books are available from amazon and Amberwaves mail order.

EDWARD ESKO BOOKS ON AMAZON

Yin Yang Primer
Contemporary Macrobiotics
Rice Field Essays
Dandelion Essays
Ki: The Energy of Life
Opening Your Third Eye
The Next Twenty Years

With Wendy Esko
Macrobiotic Cooking for Everyone

With Michio Kushi
Natural Healing through Macrobiotics
Other Dimensions
Nine Star Ki
The Macrobiotic Approach to Cancer
Forgotten Worlds
Holistic Health through Macrobiotics
Healing Harvest
Spiritual Journey
The Philosopher's Stone
Raising Healthy Kids
Basic Shiatsu
Dream Diagnosis

With Alex Jack
Cool Fusion
Corking the Nuclear Genie
The Rice Revolution

Edited By Edward Esko
Cancer and Heart Disease
Crime and Diet
Doctors Look at Macrobiotics
The Teachings of Michio Kushi
Remembering Michio

MACROBIOTICCLASSROOM.COM

Download lectures on a wide range of topics with emphasis on the macrobiotic approach to health and healing. Pursue your studies online with Edward Esko.

MP3 Audio Downloads
Free Lectures ✦ Basic Studies ✦ Foundations of Healing ✦ Advanced Healing

PDF Book Downloads
Dandelion Essays ✦ Contemporary Macrobiotics ✦ Rice Field Essays ✦ Nine Star Ki

MACROBIOTICCLASSROOM.COM
109 Wendell Ave., Pittsfield, Mass. 01201
(413) 442-1360
edwardesko@gmail.com